Love Is Now

Love Is Now

The Moods of Love Today
Edited by James Morgan
Designed by Harv Gariety

♔ HALLMARK CROWN EDITIONS

Love Is Now

You've been there, you remember:

That special place where once—
Just once—in your crowded sunlit lifetime,
You hid away in shadows from the
    tyranny of time.
That spot beside the clover
Where someone's hand held your hand,
And love was sweeter than the berries,
Or the honey,
Or the stinging taste of mint....

Tom Jones from The Fantasticks

4

It doesn't matter who you love or how you love

...but that you love.

Rod McKuen

Sweep the house clean,
hang fresh curtains
in the windows,
put on a new dress
and come with me!

The elm is scattering
its little loaves
of sweet smells
from a white sky!

Who shall hear of us
in the time to come?
Let him say there was
a burst of fragrance
from black branches.

William Carlos Williams

The first kiss — it is the union of two fragrant flowers; and the mingling of their fragrance toward the creation of a third soul.

Kahlil Gibran

Please

Do you think of me

as often as I think

of you?

Richard Brautigan

I loved you, loved you, with your unseen eyes
Sweet to my lips in nearness of night,
Sweet to my fingers that were trembling light
Upon your face to prove my true surmise
Of eyes that opened, witnessing with mine.
There had been no sign at all nor ray of sight,
But only love to prompt my guess aright...
Then dawn revealed you slowly line by line.

At first I held away your dreaming face
From my face. Till the dark blue light was keen,
Still, still I held it—though my passion beat
For it. And then all heaven on that place
Came down, since nothing ever to be seen
Again could hide your eyes, so wild, so sweet!

Witter Bynner

He came into my life as the warm wind of spring
had awakened flowers, as the April showers awaken
the earth. My love for him was an unchanging love,
high and deep, free and faithful, strong as death....

Anna Chennault

I have so little art.
Words leap from me with incoherent eagerness,
Or stumble out, stammering and vague;
Even my dumb tears gesture without eloquence.

I am so poor in gifts.
I have so few light-hearted hours,
So little fantasy to lead you on strange quests,
So little beauty to refresh your eye.

But I am great in this:
For you I hold infinities of love.
For you I am
The tender fortress of content,
The radiant harbor of desire.

Jean Starr Untermeyer

We are where love has come to live.

C. Day Lewis

They are in the time of life ... when each touch, each look, each sigh arises from the heart, the heart alone.... For them love is without thought, as to draw breath, to sleep, to walk.

Elizabeth Spencer

Here
hold my hand
let me touch you
there is
nothing
we can
say . . . your
soul
eludes me
when I reach
out
your eyes
resent
my need to know
you

here
hold my hand
since
there is nothing
we can
say

Mari Evans

We feel love as we feel the warmth of our blood, we breathe love as we breathe the air, we hold it in ourselves as we hold our thoughts. Nothing more exists for us. Love is not a word; it is a wordless state indicated by four letters.

Guy de Maupassant

I'll let you be in my dream
if I can be in yours.

Bob Dylan

I'm alone now

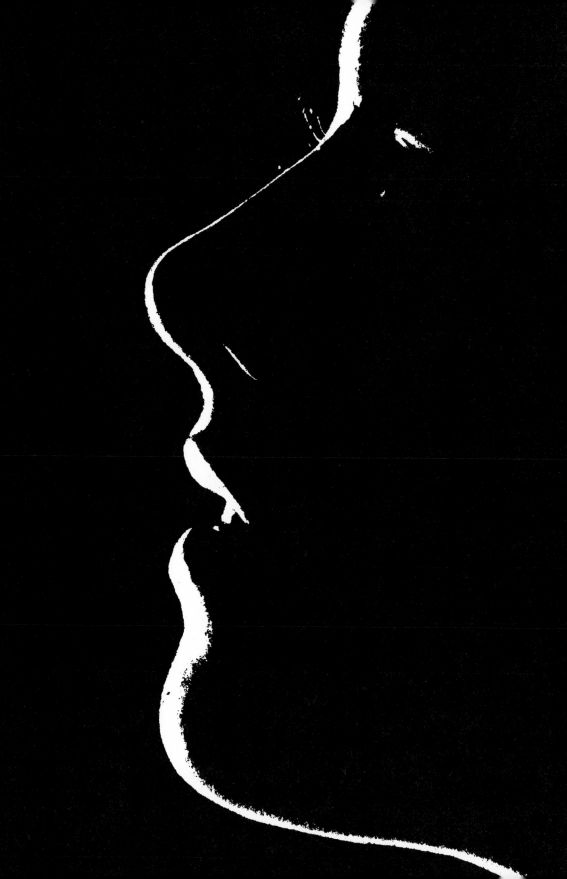

But I can touch your perfect body with my mind.

Larry Bowser

in love
we are drawn in a long curve
like the rising of light
across the photographed globe

in love
we taste other mouths
indifferent

original
in every earthly touch
in love we repeat motions
we repeat love
we repeat our rising of love
like the fierce scanning of light
across the moving earth

Joyce Carol Oates

How could you expect me
to live without you?

One cannot become accustomed
to the loss of happiness.

Gustave Flaubert

Then wear the gold hat, if that will move her;   If you can bounce high, bounce for her too

Till she cry "Lover, gold-hatted, high-bouncing lover,   I must have you!"

F. Scott Fitzgerald

Love. The feeling is too big for the word.

Elizabeth Page

The sun is up,
the sky is blue.
It's beautiful
and so are you.

John Lennon/Paul McCartney

I'll Think of You

by Naomi Sheldon

If I'm ever wondering what is love, I'll think of how much I think of you.

And if I'm ever afraid that I love too much, too soon, I'll think of you then, too, though I don't think it could happen quite like that again.

I'll remember the night I first saw you when you had to leave with the girl but came back to say How Can I Reach You.

I'll think of you on long airplane trips to sad places, and to happy places— and when I see mountains, and when the air smells of spruce.

If anyone ever brings me a book of poetry, I'll think of you because you did.

And if I ever ride a bike on a dirt road, up and down hills in the rain, I'll think of you—riding with one hand, a bottle of wine in the other.

When I'm aching from the inability to communicate, I'll think of you and how much we cared and how deeply we felt all those times when we seemed to be strangers.

If I send or receive a telegram, I'll think of you because when I tapped a message on your knee, though neither of us knew the code, you knew it said I love you.

And when it's late and I'm alone and about to get some fruit or tea, I'll think of the night I was hungry and went for some berries and the phone rang before I could wash them. It was you, and after we hung up, I put the berries back and went to sleep, warm and full.

I'll remember your saying that you wanted to love and be loved but that you were afraid. Your voice was lower and more tired than usual. I don't think I said a word.

If ever I'm frustrated by bickering, I'll
think of when I trembled for us after
our first argument and you said it was
all right, that we had to experience it in
order to get out of it. And we promised
to talk if it happened again, if we were
sad or afraid. To talk and feel instead
of trying to hide from it and ending
up fighting—longing for love, for
understanding, and fearing the longing.

And if I ever feel bad about talking too
much, I'll remember that you don't
mind, that you understand. When I
need to talk, you talk as much as I
by listening.

When I walk up long narrow stairways,
I'll think of you walking ahead of me
with your arm behind your back,
your hand holding mine, leading me
to your home.

When I'm warm I'll think of you.

And when it's cold, I'll think of you.

When I'm feeling frightened, I'll remember your saying Me Too.

If I'm ever sad because I'm not loved, I'll think of you that night at the concert saying you were afraid to love me because it would be so much.

And when I think of how huge the world is, I'll think of you and know that I exist.

Now when I play my guitar in the morning, I'll think of you asleep and smiling.

When I drink Sangria I'll think of you.

When I drink orange juice I'll think of you, toasting To Us at breakfast, our arms entwined.

I'll think of you when I'm leaving and have to think of what to say, if something must be said, so as not to say Goodbye.

When I have a birthday, I'll think of you. And when I'm on a picnic.

And if I ever feel that bodies are awkward and distant, I'll remember how ours aren't. How with us, touching is no different from smiling.

Whenever I feel alone and scared, I'll remember how you in your sleep once sensed my fear, my inanimate trembling and sorrow, and you reached for me and held me, still asleep.

When I hear the word *Baby*, sometimes so misused, I'll remember how you brought me to your chest, your arms around me, your hand on my head, and you called me Baby. It was the warmest thing I had ever heard.

I'll remember that you kissed me goodnight on my lips gently as falling asleep. I had wondered if you liked me, and found out that you loved me.

And when I'm wondering if I'm really alone, I'll remember that finally I can be with you and not have to touch you to know you are there.

When I'm wondering what I am, I'll remember the night, lying beside you, I asked you if you thought I was strange, and you said no, I wasn't, that I wasn't at all, and if you touched me then, it was gentle, and I believed you.

When I wake up in the morning and don't remember the night or my dreams, but just feel warm and peaceful and deep, I'll think of you.

And if I ever think love is futile, I'll think of you and know that love is all that matters. Futility is only a guess, a despair, but love is everything and worth all the risks.

What our love has done for us
I cannot even begin to speak
Without trembling.
You and I have left a fading world
Smog-crushed, power-crowded, dust-spun...
You and I have left this kind of world
For an infinite one:
Spinning our circles of earth and moon into galaxies
And hurling our lives into light years of reveries.
I have only begun to envision our possible place:
A someday miracle of eternal time and space.
Though it begins with such immediate smiles: your eyes
A leaf, your lips on my cheek...
Its promise is so boundless, love
I dare not speak.

Marilyn McMeen Miller

My lover, make me wholly yours
   in all the ways there are,
so a sweet bondage more endures
   than either lock or bar;

So that I never leave your breast
   to dream of other things,
but find in you my end-of-quest,
   my comfort...and my wings.

Florence Jacobs

Love Is.

Gertrude Stein

I can't remember the date
or what you wore
or what the weather was like
on the day we met.
I only remember
that you said hello
in a voice that sounded
like love.

Dean Walley

We go out together into the staring
   town
And buy cheese and bread
   and little jugs with flowered labels

Everywhere is a tent for us to put on
   our whirling show

A great deal has been said of the
   handless serpents
Which war has set loose in the gay milk
   of our heads

But because you braid your hair
   and taste like honey of heaven
We go together into town
   and buy wine and yellow candles

O this is celebration enough
   for twenty worlds!

Kenneth Patchen

More than a year has passed
Since you and I
Parted in grief and tears.

Today at last
A letter came,
One tiny, narrow sheet.

Tonight I've lit my lamp
A hundred times
To read its words of love.

Lin I Ning
Ch'ing Dynasty

There is a touch of two hands that foils all dictionaries.

Carl Sandburg

And this is love: two souls
That freely meet, and have
No need of proving anything.

Paula Reingold

I do my thing,
And you do your thing.
I am not in this world
To live up to your expectations,
And you are not in this world
To live up to mine.

You are you.
And I am I

And if by chance we find each other

It's beautiful

If not,
It can't be helped.

Fritz Perls

True love has a
language all its own.
It whispers to us
with eyes and lips and hands.
It speaks to us
with silence.

Julia Summers

And the flowers that we planted
In the seasons past will bloom
On the day you return.

Joan Baez

O love, my world is you!

Christina Rossetti

Oh, what a love it was, utterly free, unique, like
nothing else on earth! Their thoughts were like
other people's songs. . . . They loved each other
because everything around them willed it, the trees
and the clouds and the sky over their heads and
the earth under their feet. . . .

Never, never, even in their moments of
richest and wildest happiness, were they unaware
of a sublime joy in the total design of the
universe, a feeling that they themselves were a
part of that whole, an element in the beauty
of the cosmos.

Boris Pasternak
from Doctor Zhivago

Everything
is easy,
'cause of you.

Graham Nash

Falling in love appeared to me to be a special gift; I accepted the capability as I might have accepted a sense of smell suddenly heightened so that objects ordinarily scentless—hummingbirds, stones, ladybugs, clouds, tree bark, dust—became overpoweringly fragrant.

Jessamyn West

Sometimes a crumb falls
From the tables of joy,
Sometimes a bone
Is flung.

To some people
Love is given.
To others
Only heaven.

Langston Hughes

When you came, you were like red wine and honey,
And the taste of you burnt my mouth with its sweetness.
Now you are like morning bread,
Smooth and pleasant.
I hardly taste you at all, for I know your savor;
But I am completely nourished.

Amy Lowell

PHOTOGRAPHERS

Jim Cozad *page 22, 31*

Richard Fanolio *page 24, 37R, 52, 53, 64L*

Harv Gariety *page 10, 14, 18, 23 upper L, 26, 50R, 64R*

Elizabeth Gee *page 6, 8 & 9, 16 & 17, 27, 30, 45, 46, 47, 48 & 49, 54, 55*

Carol Hale *page 19*

Carter Hamilton *page 12L, 13L, 37L, 68*

Phoebe Dunn *page 58 & 59*

Maxine Jacobs and Phil Smith *page 20 & 21, 40*

Jack Jonathan *page 12R, 13R, 28, 36*

Michael McClue *page 7, 23R, 42 & 43, 62 & 63; Insert*

Sue Morey *page 44*

Rhoda Nathans *page 66 & 67*

Larry Nicholsen *page 23 lower L, 34 & 35, 50L, 51*

Herb Spencer *page 29, 60*

James Warner *page 61*

Sam Zarember *page 1, 4 & 5, 25, 32 & 33, 41, 56, 65, 69, Dust Jacket*